KID SCIENTIST

Insect Experts in the Rain Forest

Sue Fliess
illustrated by Mia Powell

Albert Whitman & Company
Chicago, Illinois

To Walter, for showing us the
Costa Rican rain forest—SF

Be kind to all kinds,
no matter how small.—MP

Library of Congress Cataloging-in-Publication data
is on file with the publisher.

Illustrations by Mia Powell
First published in the United States of America
in 2022 by Albert Whitman & Company
ISBN 978-0-8075-4147-0 (hardcover)
ISBN 978-0-8075-4148-7 (ebook)

Printed in China
10 9 8 7 6 5 4 3 2 1 WKT 26 25 24 23 22

Design by Mary Freelove

For more information about Albert Whitman & Company,
visit our website at www.albertwhitman.com.

"Let's find some ants!" Simone says to her team of entomologists as their plane lands in Costa Rica.

The team gathers their gear and boards a bus for the rain forest.

Entomologists are insect experts—they find, identify, and study insects to better understand them. Recently, a Costa Rican nature reserve invited Simone's team to investigate some army ants that appeared to have not one but two abdomens. Since no one's ever heard of ants like this before, the team jumped at the chance.

“We’ll need to find the army ant colony,” says Simone, “then figure out if these ants are a new type of ant within the same species found in this area or a new ant species altogether. My hypothesis, or guess based on our research, is that we are about to introduce a completely new ant to the world.”

Discovering a new insect species is a dream for any entomologist!

"Whatever happens," says Juliette, "I'm excited about everything we might see here. Especially if I can sketch a Costa Rican katydid."

"I hope to spot an owl butterfly," says Asher.

Majeet adds, "I want to photograph a red-legged grasshopper."

When they arrive at the park, a guide from the reserve greets them.

"My name is Walter," he says. "I'll be taking you through the park to try to find the army ant colony. Right now, the ants are in their nomadic phase, which means the colony is moving from place to place looking for food."

"How did the ants you saw act differently than regular army ants?" Simone asks.

"We noticed that these particular ants stayed at the end of the ant line, or parade," says Walter.

The team heads out, stopping occasionally to look at plants, insects, and animals or to collect samples.

"It's so full of life here," says Juliette.
"Big and small," says Majeet.

From time to time, Asher collects a sample with a sweep net, a bag-shaped tool used to gather ground vegetation.

Simone looks through the greenery carefully but finds no ants. "Even if we don't see the ants today," she says, "we have enough samples to study until tomorrow."

"Like this urania swallowtail moth," replies Juliette, lifting her collecting jar.

After a full day of exploring, the team begins packing to leave.

"Look!" says Majeet, pointing out army ants marching over his boot. "Are *these* our ants?"

Simone checks out the end of the ant parade. "These ants look like they have two abdomens!"

"Those are the ones!" shouts Walter.

The team observes the ants.

Then Simone uses a pooter, a device used to collect insects for observation, to suck a few of the unusual ants through a tube and into a container.

“Don’t worry,” she tells Walter. “This doesn’t hurt insects, and it makes it easier to study them up close.”

At the reserve's lab the next morning, Majeet uploads his photos, and Juliette scans in her sketches. Asher types up notes, and Simone examines one of the strange ants.

“This ant sure looks like it has two abdomens,” says Simone. “Come see.”

"Can you flip the ant over?" suggests Asher.

Simone gently moves the ant, and they watch as something falls off of its abdomen.

"Hold on. That's a beetle!" says Simone. "The ant didn't have a second abdomen. It had a beetle attached to it."

"The beetle was getting a piggyback ride," laughs Majeet.

"And because the beetle is the same size, shape, and color as the ant's abdomen, we couldn't tell," says Juliette.

"It appears the beetle was mimicking the ant's abdomen," says Simone.

The scientists photograph the ant and the beetle, then watch as the beetle reattaches itself to the ant.

"The beetle uses its powerful mandibles, or mouthparts, to attach itself to the ant's waist," observes Simone.

"But why?" asks Asher.

"Great question," replies Simone. "Let's talk about what we know."

"Army ants travel in big colonies for safety from enemies," says Majeet.

"And army ants don't have permanent nests," says Juliette. "They only stop moving so the queen can lay eggs."

"Then, once they have larvae, or babies, to feed, the colony roams around again, looking for food," adds Asher.

“Based on this information,” says Simone, “I have a new hypothesis. The beetles travel with the colony for protection from enemies and for easy access to food.”

“Free protection, a free ride, *and* free food!” says Asher.

“Lots of species rely on army ants to survive,” says Majeet. “But I’ve never heard about an insect possibly mimicking an ant’s abdomen before! Does this mean we’ve found a new way insects camouflage themselves to survive?”

"Maybe," says Simone. "But we'll need to do more research to confirm our hypotheses."

The team spends the rest of the day reading scientific studies on beetles in Costa Rica.

Finally, Simone announces, “Congratulations, team. This beetle has not been identified yet. We thought we came here to identify a new ant, but instead we’ve just discovered a new species of Costa Rican beetle!”

The team celebrates before making plans to share their findings with entomologists everywhere. With the help of park guides, they will continue studying the beetle's role in the Costa Rican ecosystem and write their report.

“It always amazes me,” says Simone, “how such a tiny thing can lead to a big discovery.”

WHAT IS AN ENTOMOLOGIST?

Entomologists study insects' anatomy, habitats, life cycles, and behaviors. Their job includes locating and identifying insects so people can better understand and classify them.

Insects are defined as animals with six legs and antennae. Most have two or four wings, hatch from eggs, and have segmented bodies and limbs with joints. Insects have been around for millions of years, and scientists believe there may be more than 35 million types of insects living today.

All scientists research by following the steps of the scientific method. Simone and her team used each step to guide their research.

STEPS OF THE SCIENTIFIC METHOD

1. Make observations and do background research. Before Simone and her team traveled to Costa Rica, they did research on native insects, in particular the army ant.
2. Ask questions about your observations and gather information. After hearing about the ants, Simone asked Walter how the ants' appearances differed from regular army ants and what behaviors the ants were displaying.
3. Form a hypothesis. Originally, Simone hypothesized that this was a new species of army ant. After discovering the beetles, she hypothesized why they would latch onto army ants.
4. Perform an experiment and collect data. Simone and her team gathered vegetation samples with sweep nets and collected individual army ants with a pooter suction tool.
5. Analyze the data and draw conclusions. Consider how the conclusions support or disprove your hypothesis. Once the team had a chance to examine the army ants up close, they realized beetles were riding on the ants. This discovery led them to identify a new species of beetle instead of a new species of ant. The team then formed a new hypothesis about why the beetles attached themselves to the ants.
6. Communicate or present your findings. After gathering more data, Simone and her team will publish their research so others can learn about this new species of Costa Rican beetle.

HOW CAN I BECOME AN ENTOMOLOGIST?

Do insects fascinate you? Maybe you'll become an entomologist!

There are so many ways to study insects, even before you decide on a career:

- Check out books at your local library or visit a nearby zoo's insect exhibit.
- Go outside and look in the grass, shrubs, or nearby fields, or check tree bark and branches for insects. You might find caterpillars, butterflies, roly-poly bugs, ants, or even beetles.
- Take a nature hike and bring a camera and a magnifying glass.
- Buy your own pooter tool (they're inexpensive), and with the help of a grown up, collect some insects to gently observe before releasing them back into their habitat.
- Use a butterfly net and a clear jar with a screw-on lid to capture insects safely. An adult can help you put air holes in the lid so the insects can breathe. When you are done observing your insects, let them go.

When you're older, you can choose a college that offers a bachelor of science degree in Entomology or a related field in the biological sciences.

You might then go on to have a career in agriculture or biological or genetic research. Some entomologists research how to control insect-borne diseases or prevent crop damage by insects. Others teach or have jobs in ecology, forestry, medicine, and other fields. There are many jobs you can do as an entomologist! Maybe you'll even be a member of the Entomological Society of America.

MORE TO READ

Honovich, Nancy. *1,000 Facts about Insects*. Washington, DC: National Geographic, 2018.

Koontz, Robin. *Entomologists*. Vero Beach, FL: Rourke, 2016.

Murphy, Patricia J. *Investigating Insects with a Scientist*. Berkeley Heights, NJ: Enslow, 2004.

Young, Karen Romano. *Bug Science: 20 Projects and Experiments about Arthropods: Insects, Arachnids, Algae, Worms, and Other Small Creatures*. Washington, DC: National Geographic, 2009.

Author's Note: This story is loosely based on a true event from 2014, when two biologists, Christoph von Beeren and Daniel Kronauer of Technical University Darmstadt, Germany, discovered a new species of beetle that was hitching a ride on army ants in Costa Rica, making the ants appear to have two abdomens. They named the beetle Nymphister kronaueri.